HURRICANE!

by Elizabeth Field

illustrated by Lane Yerkes

Harcourt

Orlando   Boston   Dallas   Chicago   San Diego

Visit *The Learning Site!*

www.harcourtschool.com

While Tony and Tina were playing checkers, the weather forecast came on. A hurricane was only a few hundred miles away.

"Hurricanes begin over the ocean," said Tony. "Sometimes they travel toward land. If they reach the coast, the heavy wind and rain can cause awful damage."

"How do people get ready?"
asked Tina.

"One thing people do is protect their boats so they will not drift away in the rough sea," said Tony.

Tina wondered what would happen if a fleet of boats drifted out to sea.

"Let's do an experiment," said Tony.
He filled the bathtub with water. He
and Tina launched a fleet of plastic
boats in the tub.

The boats drifted slowly. Then Tony and Tina blew hard to make a strong wind. The boats crashed into each other, and some of them sank!

"Sometimes people must leave
their homes before a hurricane comes,"
said Tony.

"Their homes may not be safe
when the heavy rain and strong
winds arrive."

The weather forecasters were still
talking about the hurricane, which was
named Hector. The storm would not
pass Tony and Tina's house, but it
wouldn't be too far away.

When a hurricane forms over the Atlantic Ocean, it is given a name. Both male and female names are used. Here is the list for the year 2001.

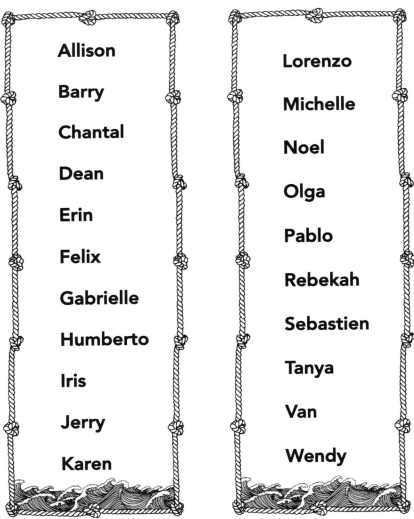

Allison

Barry

Chantal

Dean

Erin

Felix

Gabrielle

Humberto

Iris

Jerry

Karen

Lorenzo

Michelle

Noel

Olga

Pablo

Rebekah

Sebastien

Tanya

Van

Wendy

"Is the storm coming here?"
Tina asked.

"No," Tony said, "but it will be windy
and rainy tonight and tomorrow."

outer bands of rain

eye of the hurricane

Hurricanes are large storms. Bands of rain and wind spread out over a wide area. The outer bands have the weakest wind and the least rain.

Dark clouds were now looming in the sky. The children realized that some of the storm would come their way.

"We're lucky we don't live on the coast," said Tony.

"What would we do if we lived on the coast?" Tina asked.

"We would have to leave our house and drive to a place that was safe from the storm."

That evening, the winds blew and the rain came, but Tony and Tina didn't care. They knew they were safe in their cozy home.